First Facts™

Animal Behavior

Animals Staying Safe

by Xavier Niz

Capstone
press

Mankato, Minnesota

First Facts is published by Capstone Press
151 Good Counsel Drive, P.O. Box 669, Mankato, Minnesota 56002
www.capstonepress.com

Library of Congress Cataloging-in-Publication Data
Niz, Xavier.
    Animals staying safe / by Xavier Niz.
    p. cm.—(First facts. Animal behavior)
    Includes bibliographical references (p. 23) and index.
    ISBN 0-7368-2627-0 (hardcover)
    1. Animal defenses—Juvenile literature. I. Title. II. Series.
QL759.N59 2005
591.47—dc22   2004000328

Summary: Discusses the ways that animals defend and protect themselves from danger.

Editorial Credits
Gillia Olson, editor; Jennifer Bergstrom, series designer; Linda Clavel, book designer;
    Kelly Garvin, photo researcher; Eric Kudalis, product planning editor

Photo Credits
Bernd Heinrich, 8
Bruce Coleman Inc./Hans Reinhard, 12–13; Jen & Des Bartlett, 5; Laura Riley, 16–17
James P. Rowan, 9
Jeff Rotman, 10
Minden Pictures/Fred Bavendam, 20; Jim Brandenburg, 14
Robert McCaw, 6–7, 11
Seapics.com/David B. Fleetham, cover
Tom & Pat Leeson, 15
Tom Stack & Associates Inc./Dave B. Fleetham, 19

**First Facts thanks Bernd Heinrich, PhD, Department of Biology, University of Vermont in
Burlington, Vermont, for his assistance in reviewing this book.**

1 2 3 4 5 6 09 08 07 06 05 04

Table of Contents

A Skunk's Protection

A skunk makes its way across a snowy field. Suddenly, a coyote appears. To **defend** itself, the skunk sprays a stinky liquid. The liquid hits the coyote in the face. Tears fill the coyote's eyes. The coyote starts to feel sick. The skunk gets away.

! Fun Fact!
Skunks have good aim. Skunks can spray on target from as far as 12 feet (3.7 meters) away.

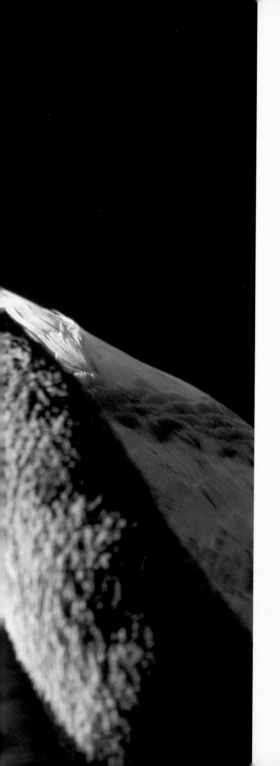

Safe in the Wild

In the wild, animals must **protect** themselves. Some animals blend into their surroundings. Some use tricky moves to escape **predators**. Some build strong homes to keep out predators. Other animals work together to stay safe.

Fun Fact!
Many birds, including the trumpeter swan, sleep with one eye open to watch for danger.

Appearance

Some animals use their **appearance** to stay safe. The gray tree frog blends in with the tree bark where it lives. Predators might not see the frog.

The polyphemus moth has spots
on its wings. The spots look like eyes.
Predators might mistake the moth for
a large animal and stay away.

Tricky Moves

Some animals use tricky moves to stay safe. An octopus shoots out a dark liquid when it is attacked. The liquid hides the octopus, letting it escape.

A skink can break off its tail to escape a predator. The tail flops around. It **distracts** the predator. Over time, the skink will grow a new tail.

Strong Homes

Some animals build strong homes to stay safe. Some termites build their homes by mixing soil and **saliva**. This mixture hardens to be very strong. Predators have a tough time breaking into the mounds.

> **! Fun Fact!**
> Termite mounds can be 20 feet (6.1 meters) high.

13

Working Together

Some animals protect each other.
Musk oxen form a circle around their
young when predators come near. The
adults stand with their horns outward.

A group of crows will sometimes attack an eagle or other predator. The crows fly around and make noise. The crows chase the predator away.

Keeping the Peace

Animals sometimes face danger from their own kind. Wolves may fight over food or **territory**. To avoid a fight, a wolf crouches down. The wolf turns down its ears. It may also whine.

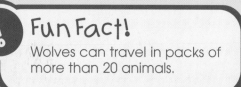

Fun Fact!
Wolves can travel in packs of more than 20 animals.

Staying Safe

Animals have many ways to stay safe. Tree frogs blend in with tree bark. Termites build strong homes. Musk oxen stick together when attacked. How do you think this porcupine fish stays safe?

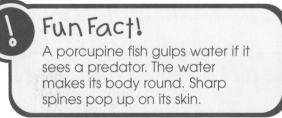

Fun Fact!

A porcupine fish gulps water if it sees a predator. The water makes its body round. Sharp spines pop up on its skin.

19

Amazing but True!

Sometimes, different kinds of animals protect each other. Goby fish and snapping shrimp share the same home. Outside their home, the shrimp touches the goby's body. If the goby sees danger, it signals the shrimp. Both the goby and the shrimp swim quickly back to their home.

Hands On: Blending In

Many animals use coloring to protect themselves from predators. Some animals have body shapes or patterns of colors that help them blend in with their surroundings. Try this activity to see how animals use coloring to help them hide.

What You Need

piece of white construction paper
blunt-end scissors
crayons or markers
a friend

What You Do

1. Draw a frog on the construction paper.
2. Cut out the frog with the scissors.
3. Locate an area where you want to hide your frog. It could be on the sofa, on the kitchen table, or on a book.
4. Using crayons or markers, color your frog to match the hiding place.
5. Have a friend try to find your animal in its surroundings.

Glossary

appearance (uh-PIHR-uhnss)—the way something looks

defend (di-FEND)—to stop an attack

distract (diss-TRAKT)—to draw attention away from something

predator (PRED-uh-tur)—an animal that hunts other animals for food

protect (pruh-TEKT)—to keep something safe

saliva (suh-LYE-vuh)—the clear liquid in the mouth

territory (TER-uh-tor-ee)—an area of land an animal claims as its own

Read More

Hoff, Mary King. *Mimicry and Camouflage.* World of Wonder. Mankato, Minn.: Creative Education, 2003.

Taylor, Barbara. *Scary and Sneaky.* The Natural History Museum Weird and Wonderful Guides. Chicago: Peter Bedrick Books, 2001.

Internet Sites

FactHound offers a safe, fun way to find Internet sites related to this book. All of the sites on FactHound have been researched by our staff.

Here's how:
1. Visit *www.facthound.com*
2. Type in this special code **0736826270** for age-appropriate sites. Or enter a search word related to this book for a more general search.
3. Click on the **Fetch It** button.

FactHound will fetch the best sites for you!

Index